LEARN

Spanish

WORDS

grandmother
la abuela
(lah ah-boo-EH-lah)

grandfather
el abuelo
(el ah-boo-EH-loh)

sister
la hermana
(lah er-MAH-nah)

mother
la madre
(lah MAH-dreh)

father
el padre
(el PAH-dreh)

cake
el pastel
(el pas-TEL)

presents
los regalos
(lohs re-GAH-lohs)

BY M. J. YORK • ILLUSTRATED BY KATHLEEN PETELINSEK

Published by The Child's World®
1980 Lookout Drive • Mankato, MN 56003-1705
800-599-READ • www.childsworld.com

Acknowledgments
The Child's World®: Mary Berendes, Publishing Director
Translator: Silvia Amigo Silvestre, Senior Lecturer of Spanish
Language, Cornell University
The Design Lab: Design
Red Line Editorial: Editorial direction
Amnet: Production

ISBN 9781626873797
LCCN 2014930629

Printed in the United States of America
Mankato, MN
July, 2014
PA02217

ABOUT THE AUTHOR

M. J. York is a children's author and editor living in Minnesota. She loves learning about different people and places.

ABOUT THE ILLUSTRATOR

Kathleen Petelinsek loves to draw and paint. She also loves to travel to exotic countries where people speak foreign languages. She lives in Minnesota with her husband, two daughters, two dogs, a fluffy cat, and three chickens.

CONTENTS

Introduction to Spanish

Spanish is one of the most common languages in the world. It has at least 358 million speakers. Many Spanish speakers live in North and South America. They live in Spain and the Philippines, too. Mexico has the most Spanish speakers of any country.

Spanish is a Romance language. Romance languages grew out of Latin, the language spoken by the ancient Romans. French, Italian, and Portuguese are Romance languages too.

Spanish is a little different in each country where it is spoken. Some phrases are different. Some things are pronounced differently. But people can still understand each other. This book shows how the Spanish words are pronounced in Latin America.

Spanish uses the same alphabet as English. Spanish has a few more letters, though. Most are pronounced the same way, but a few are different.

h [ ] is always silent

j [h] like h as in *hot*

ll [y] like y as in *yes*

ñ [ny] like ny as in *año* (an-yo)

qu [k] like k as in *Kate*

r [r] like r as in *road*, but trilled or rolled

rr [rr] always strongly trilled

v [b] like b as in *boat*

The vowels always make the same sound. They are:

a [ah] like a as in *father*

e [eh] like e as in *feather*

i [ee] like ee as in *see*

o [oh] like o as in *long*

u [oo] like oo as in *food*

Sometimes a vowel has an accent mark: á, é, í, ó, ú. The accent mark shows that syllable is stressed.

My Home
Mi casa
(me KAH-sah)

window
la ventana
(lah ven-TAH-nah)

lamp
la lámpara
(lah LAM-pah-rah)

bathroom
el baño
(el BA-nyo)

bedroom
la habitación
(la ah-bee-tah-see-ON)

television
la televisión
(lah teh-leh-vee-see-ON)

kitchen
la cocina
(lah ko-SEE-nah)

cat
el gato
(el GAH-toh)

living room
el salón
(el sah-LON)

sofa
el sofá
(el soh-FAH)

chair
la silla
(lah SEE-yah)

table
la mesa
(lah MEH-sah)

In the Morning
Por la mañana
(por lah mah-NYAH-nah)

dresser
la cómoda
(lah KOH-moh-dah)

clock
el reloj
(el reh-LHOH)

teddy bear
el osito
(el oh-SEE-toh)

doll
la muñeca
(lah moo-NYEH-kah)

pillow
la almohada
(lah al-moh-AH-dah)

bed
la cama
(lah KAH-mah)

blanket
la manta
(lah MAN-tah)

At the Park
En el parque
(en el PAR-keh)

Let's play!
¡Vamos a jugar!
(VAH-mohs ah hoo-GAR!)

sky
el cielo
(el SEE-EH-loh)

friend (male)
el amigo
(el ah-MEE-goh)

friend (female)
la amiga
(lah ah-MEE-gah)

soccer ball
el balón de fútbol
(el bah-LON deh FOOT-ball)

bird
el pájaro
(el PAH-hah-roh)

MORE USEFUL WORDS

board game
un juego
(oon HOO-EH-go)

sports game
un partido
(oon par-TEE-doh)

sports
los deportes
(lohs deh-POR-tehs)

sun
el sol
(el sol)

swing
el columpio
(el ko-LOOM-pee-oh)

clouds
las nubes
(lahs NOO-behs)

playground
el parque
(el PAR-keh)

slide
el tobogán
(el toh-boh-GAN)

water
el agua
(el AH-goo-ah)

pond
el estanque
(el es-TAN-keh)

flower
la flor
(lah FLOR)

duck
el pato
(el PAH-toh)

13

airplane
el avión
(el ah-vee-ON)

office
la oficina
(lah oh-fee-SEE-nah)

building
el edificio
(el eh-dee-FEE-see-oh)

2100 OFFICE BUILDING

bus
el autobus
(el ow-toh-BOOS)

CITY BUS

MORE USEFUL WORDS

truck
la camioneta
(lah kah-mee-oh-NEH-tah)

train
el tren
(el TREN)

stop
pare
(PAH-reh)

go
camine
(kah-MEEH-neh)

15

My Birthday Party
Mi fiesta de cumpleaños
(meeh fee-ES-tah deh koom-ple-AH-nyos)

grandmother
la abuela
(lah ah-boo-EH-lah)

grandfather
el abuelo
(el ah-boo-EH-loh)

I am six years old.
Tengo seis años.
(TEN-go SEH-ees AH-nyo)

brother
el hermano
(el er-MAH-no)

sister
la hermana
(lah er-MAH-nah)

cake
el pastel
(el pas-TEL)

MORE USEFUL WORDS

one **uno** *(OO-noh)*	eleven **once** *(ON-seh)*
two **dos** *(dose)*	twelve **doce** *(DOH-seh)*
three **tres** *(trehs)*	thirteen **trece** *(TREH-seh)*
four **cuatro** *(koo-AH-troh)*	fourteen **catorce** *(kah-TOR-seh)*
five **cinco** *(SEEN-koh)*	fifteen **quince** *(KEEN-seh)*
six **seis** *(SEH-ees)*	sixteen **dieciséis** *(dee-eh-see-SEH-ees)*
seven **siete** *(see-EH-teh)*	seventeen **diecisiete** *(dee-eh-see-see-EH-teh)*
eight **ocho** *(OH-choh)*	eighteen **dieciocho** *(dee-eh-see-OH-choh)*
nine **nueve** *(noo-EH-beh)*	nineteen **diecinueve** *(dee-eh-see-noo-EH-beh)*
ten **diez** *(dee-EHS)*	twenty **veinte** *(veh-IN-teh)*

19

Time for Dinner
La Hora de la Cena
(lah OH-rah deh lah SEH-nah)

bread
el pan
(el pan)

stove
la estufa
(lah es-TOO-fah)

pot
la olla
(lah OH-yah)

I am hungry.
Tengo hambre.
(TEN-go AM-breh.)

glass
el vaso
(el BAH-soh)

rice
el arroz
(el ah-ROS)

meat
la carne
(lah KAR-neh)

plate
el plato
(el PLAH-toh)

knife
el cuchillo
(el koo-CHEE-yoh)

fork
el tenedor
(el ten-eh-DOR)

spoon
la cuchara
(lah koo-CHAH-rah)

At Night
Por la Noche
(por lah NO-cheh)

Good night!
¡Buenas noches!
(boo-EH-nas NO-ches!)

I feel tired (female).
Estoy cansada.
(es-TOY kan-SAH-dah.)

bathtub
la bañera
(lah bah-NYE-rah)

I feel tired (male).
Estoy cansado.
(es-TOY kan-SAH-doh.)

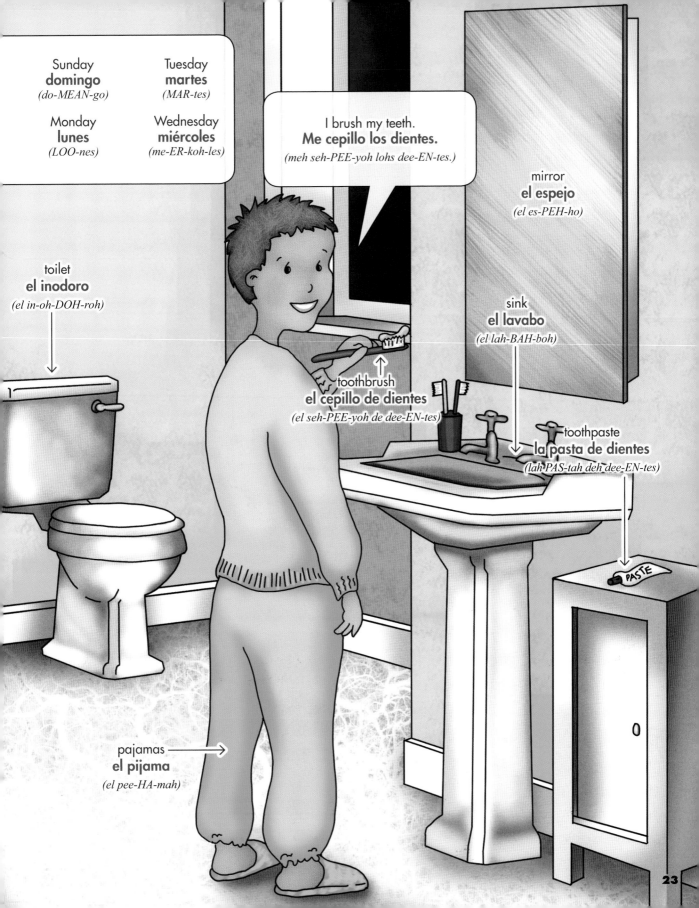

MORE USEFUL WORDS

Yes
sí
(see)

No
no
(no)

ten
diez
(dee-EHS)

twenty
veinte
(veh-IN-teh)

thirty
treinta
(TREH-in-tah)

forty
cuarenta
(koo-ah-REN-tah)

fifty
cincuenta
(seen-koo-EN-tah)

sixty
sesenta
(seh-SEN-tah)

seventy
setenta
(seh-TEN-tah)

eighty
ochenta
(oh-CHEN-tah)

ninety
noventa
(no-BEN-tah)

one hundred
cien
(see-EN)

January
enero
(en-EH-roh)

February
febrero
(feh-BRE-roh)

March
marzo
(MAR-soh)

April
abril
(AH-bril)

May
mayo
(MAH-yoh)

June
junio
(HOO-nee-oh)

July
julio
(HOO-lee-oh)

August
agosto
(ah-GOS-toh)

September
septiembre
(sep-tee-EM-breh)

October
octubre
(ok-TOO-breh)

November
noviembre
(no-bee-EM-breh)

December
diciembre
(dee-see-EM-breh)

winter
el invierno
(el in-bee-ER-noh)

spring
la primavera
(lah pri-mah-BEH-rah)

summer
el verano
(el beh-RAH-no)

fall
el otoño
(el oh-TOH-nyoh)

good-bye!
¡Adiós!
(a-dee-OHS!)